Mr. Troxel,
Is it true bacteria eat you alive when you're dead?

M.C. Troxel

Eph 2:1-10

ISBN: 1453703527

ISBN-13: 978-1453703526

This book is dedicated to Jennifer.

You started all this!

ACKNOWLEDGMENTS

Thanks to All my students over the years.

You have kept me laughing and feeling like I'm

"16 with 34 years of experience."

Thanks to my family for all your love and
encouragement.

8

Preface

For some 12 years now I have had the privilege of teaching high school in a beautiful southern town. As with any job there are days when the stress can seem unbearable. Just when you're about to scream, "I can't take it anymore!" someone pops up and says something that totally catches you off guard causing you to laugh in spite of your circumstances. Such was the case at the advent of this book. In 2002 I was having a particularly stressful day. I had a parent conference in the morning before school, it was my day for lunch duty and I was scheduled for another conference after school. Several students decided it was the "National Day of Disrespect to Teachers" and I had $25 in the checking account to make it 5 days until payday. By 7th period I was ready to put the trash can over my head and hope my students wouldn't notice me.

While the students were "working" on an assignment and I sat at my desk rubbing my eyes hoping the headache would go away, a young lady walked up to my desk with a most serious look on her face and asked in all sincerity, "Mr. Troxel, Is it true the bacteria eat you alive when you're dead?" I really tried to keep a straight face but I just couldn't help myself; the laughter burst forth and when she realized what she had just said she began to laugh with me. I turned and wrote her question on the board and it became a source of levity all the next day. I began to write the statements and questions other students made on the board and soon started recording them in what has been affectionately named by the students as "The Book". Over the years "The Book" has become somewhat famous within our school. Students I taught as freshman will come back as seniors just to read through the quotes and laugh at their own statements that "made The Book." On occasion other teachers have sent me quotes from their students. Together my students and I have learned to laugh with each other and at ourselves. This entire process has brought so much joy to my heart and our school, so I decided it was time to share it with the world. I realize that some of you cannot imagine that some of the quotes in this book could have come out of the mouths of high school students, but if you will spend a day or two observing in a high school near you, you will become a true believer. Over these pages I will attempt to set the context for the quotes, but please understand that some defy explanation. I have also written many of the words phonetically to help you understand how they were pronounced. I hope you enjoy!

M.C. Troxel

* * * * *

"I think you missed something!"

Sometimes as a teacher you realize that your students are not "getting" what you are teaching. Parents feel the same way when their progeny act as if they've never heard any word they've said. The following are examples of times students have failed to "get it". (I teach science)

After a lesson on nuclear reactions a student asked, "Couldn't soda be a type of fission?"

"Did Sir Isaac Newton invent the 'Fig Newton'?"

Me: "The space shuttle orbits the earth upside-down and backwards."

Student: "Don't planes fly like that too?"

"Is there such a thing as chicken milk? They have breasts!"

11

"I thought acceleration means like to push the gas."

"Is sugar made from salt?"

Student A: "Where are baby cows before they are born?"

Me: "In the cow's womb!"

Student B: "That's its butt!"

While I was explaining that the word Sahara means desert, so it is redundant to say Sahara Desert a student said, "Well then you should just say Sierra Desert!"

Student A: "Is there such a thing as stomach acid?"

Student B: "Yeah 'cause I got acid reflexes!"

Me: "Who developed the Law of Conservation of Mass? Hint- He's French"

Student: "Francis Marion"

(The worst part about this statement is we live in South Carolina)

Me: "Who is known as the 'father' of the Periodic Table of Elements? - He lived in Siberia!"

Student: "Oh that's that dude 'Osom ben Notlen' or whatever!"

Question during an anatomy lesson:

"Shouldn't you have to be a certain height to be pregnant? I mean wouldn't you fall over?"

Student A: "Mr.Troxel – What are aphids?"

Student B: "Those are people who don't believe in God –ain't it!"

Me: "How are molecules held together?"

Student: "By conveyor belts!"

"Spores? That's like holes in your arm!"

Me: "Frequency is given in the unit hertz."

Student: "That's ketchup!"

"Your lips are right beside your mouth!"

Me: "He has Lyme's Disease."

Student: "Mr. Troxel - Do limes really have diseases?"

On the first day of school we try to familiarize students with the safety stations in the lab. When I pointed out the eye-wash station a student asked, "Is it wireless?"

Early one morning a student asked me if I had a favorite hamburger joint. I told him about a place in North Carolina where they "Don't call them hamburgers they call them steak-burgers." The student asked, "What about the bones? Won't you choke on them?"

"Mummies can't be mummified people!"

"Do skinny people have less organs?"

"Is the moon the oldest star?"

During a lab a student was unclear about how long to keep a liquid at a certain temperature;

Student A: "How long does it stay up?"

Me: "90 Seconds!"

Student B: "I thought you said a minute and a half!?"

Student A: "Mr. T, Can't you CPR the drowning out of someone?"

Student B: "I can drown in a pool and come out alive."

Student C: "In the Navy they kill you! They water drown you to death so you know what it feels like."

After a lesson on the color spectrum a student said, "Black and white make yellow!"

Answer on a test: "Solar collectors are part of the solar system."

Instructions for the lab: "Fill the beaker with 50ml of tap water."

Student: "How do you tap water?"

"So your nerves have feelings?"

"How do you convert from feet to foot?"

"Is it true if you put a light bulb in a potato it will light up?"

"I thought arsenic was like burning down houses."

"Could you live without a neck?"

I was explaining to students that a mechanical wave is a repeating disturbance (vibration) that carries energy through a medium. A student raised her hand and asked, "Isn't a wave what's in the ocean?" I responded, "There are waves in the ocean." She said, "Then why are you teaching us wrong?"

Student: "What does AM – FM stand for?"

Me: "Amplitude Modulation and Frequency Modulation"

Student: "I thought AM was like morning music and FM was night music."

Teacher: "Rome built many aqueducts to carry water."

Student: "Do you mean 'aqua-ducks' like quack-quack?"

Student A: "What is that that will tell you if you are having a boy or a girl?"

Student B: "Chlorophyll"

Student A: "What's that animal that changes colors?"

Me: "A Chameleon"

Student B: "I thought it was a lizard!"

Me: "What's the temperature?"

Student: "It's like negative zero."

I pointed to the Periodic Table on my wall one day and asked a student, "What is this called?" (Keep in mind the words 'Periodic Table of Elements' are written in 6 inch letters at the top.) The student replied, "The Patriotic Table!"

Me: Ok, let's continue our discussion on Mendelian Genetics

Student: "Is Mendel's daughter or wife's name Mendelian?"

"So are they conjunction twins?"

Me: "The little nerve cells in your ear are like tiny hairs."

Student: "Can you shampoo them?"

"Synthetic elements... that's like a weave right?"

"MnO is almost like NOPE."

Me: "Today we are going to begin our section on Botany."

Student: "I thought Botany was like getting your face pulled back."

Me: "Potassium will react violently in water."

Student: "That's why I don't eat bananas, because I'm afraid my mouth might blow up – there's potassium in them."

Me: "A water moccasin is a venomous snake."

Student: "Nuh-un, it's a big water proof shoe."

"Sharks aren't fish they are mammals."

Me: "Even the air we breathe is made of atoms."

Student: "If you breathe in atoms why don't you choke?"

Me: "Ni is nickel on the Periodic Table."

Student: "Then where's the quarter?"

Teacher: "Give me an example of something that weighs a gram."

Student: "A teddy graham!" (Honors student)

In 2003 before the TV series "LOST": "Mr. Troxel, Could polar bears live in South America?"

Me: "Most mammals have fur..."

Student: "So those trees have fur so they are mammals?" (Fir Trees)

"Herring, isn't that a drug?"

"What sound makes that noise?"

After reading the pre-lab instruction sheet a student asked, "What's liquid water? Do we have powdered water?"

"Ammonia… I thought that was a disease or sickness."

Teacher: "He needs to write about a quarter of a page."

Student: "Not even that much, more like a third of a page."

Answer on a test:

"The cation is part of the part of the compound with a positive charge. The negative part is called an Onion." (Anion)

Teacher: "You don't know what an anvil is?"

Student A: "Advil – yeah."

Student B: "You talking about those things they put at the bottom of boats to stop it?"

* * * * *

The weather often provides some interesting observations and conclusions from students. While it may be small talk to most adults the weather seems to affect everything about the lives of young people. It even affects their ability to reason.

After getting caught in the rain:

"My head is wet, I going to get ammonia!"

Student: "I'm cold!"

Me: "It's 15 degrees outside and you're wondering why you're cold, you have on flip flops!"

Student: "Well my body's not cold just my toes!"

"My ankle hurts when the weather is changing. It's like my 3rd sense."

Student: "Mr. Troxel I was under a spell yesterday."

Me: "A spell?"

Student: "You know a heat spell from getting too hot!"

A student with a bad sunburn said, "I going to come to school skinless tomorrow!"

A student came to my desk and asked for a tissue to blow his nose. Another student said:

"He sound constipated… you know all stuff up!"

"Mr. Troxel I've got heartburn… I walked outside and that heat hit my heart and it burned."

"Only two things happen when I get allergic to pollen: My nose get all clog up or I can't breathe."

"Isn't like 30° freezing in the winter and freezing in the summer is like 70°?"

"If you close your eyes it make the room colder."

"It's a great day outside… The weather's kind of nasty though."

* * * * *

I'm a huge science fiction movie fan, especially *Star Wars,* so some students like to relate on that level. The problem is they are often NOT science fiction fans. These are particularly humorous to the nerd in me.

"I have a green lifesaver because it's Yoda!"

"Black Vader has soft skin!"

"What was that little guys name... Yogi?" (Yoda)

"Mr.T, who is your favorite 'Transformer'? Optimistic Prime?"

A student looked at my tie that said STAR WARS on it and asked, "Is that a Star Wars tie?"

* * * * *

Sometimes listening to student conversations can be very enlightening. Still other times you wish you hadn't been listening. What follows are tidbits of those things spoken by students within earshot when all their defenses were down.

"He was a twin brother but he's way older."

Student A: "My mom is sending me to Rome."

Student B: "How are you going to learn the language?"

Student A: "There's a French class in this school – Duh!"

Student A: "He never calls me back or texts me back. Not to mention every time I turn around she's over there and claims he's busy.

Student B: "Yeah, you should 'dumpling' him!"

Student A: "You would like my mom if she was alive."

Student B: "Where did she go?"

"I didn't order a cheese-steak because I don't eat meat, so I ordered a meatball sub instead."

"These egg rolls taste watered down!"

Student A: "That's child abuse! Somebody call the SPCA!"

Student B: "That's for dogs."

Student A: "Then call the S.Kid-O.A.!"

Student B: "You mean Social Services."

Student A: "Yeah BSS"

Student A: "Where did you move from?"

Student B: "California."

Student A: "Did you know a kid named Drew?"

"I'm not 'disabilitated'!"

Student A: "He got stabbed to death."

Student B: "Yeah, but he lived."

Student A: "Say the alphabet backwards."

Student B: "OK, 7, 6, 5…"

"There are 7 weeks in a month!"

Student A: "These halls are so crowded."

Student B: "Yeah, I hate upper-freshmen."

Student A: "Lance Armstrong is the guy who walked on the moon."

Student B: "No, it was Louis Armstrong."

Student C: "It's Neil Armstrong… Louis Armstrong was his brother."

Student A: "Can men have babies?

Student B: "Yes if he has the female parts!"

Student A: "Y'all know Terrell Owens tried to commit suicide yesterday?"

Student B: "No he attempted it!"

Student A: "She's a 'dramatizer'!"

Student b: "that sounds like food!"

Student A: "What kind of food?"

Student B: "Fish!"

"I made like 6 hamburgers but I had to throw 7 of them away."

Student A: "My uncle owns a dairy farm in California."

Student B: "California doesn't have cows!"

"You make me want to go to the bathroom and just … sit there!"

Student A: "I'm about to catch a heart attack!"

Student B: "Is that contagious?"

"Isn't that Hallie Berry a basketball player?"

Student A: "What are y'all doing in art?"

Student B: "We have to make paper machete!" (Dangerous art class)

"I'm afraid that horses will punch me in the face and I just found out that zebras are horses!"

I was eating some strawberry yogurt during my lunch and a student says, "I want some 'yogrit'!"

"His feet smell like – um – feet"

After being struck in the eye by a piece of paper a student shouted, "Now I'm going to be deaf!"

A young man asked a friend, "Aren't Latinos female Mexicans?"

"Wasn't Barney purple people?"

"I want to play football! I'm going to be a... what are they called?... a 'Power Puff Girl'!"

* * * * *

It is said that truth often flows "out of the mouths of babes." In the classroom, students will blurt out statements without much tact or thought and often their logic is hard to refute. (That's if there is any logic at all)

My student volunteer asked, Mr.T, What did you do that was new and different over the weekend?" I said, "I used ear candles this weekend." She replied, "If you had enough wax in your ears to make candles something has got to be wrong."

"Mr. Troxel, Do only teachers get AIDS? I always hear about teacher's aides."

"If you can't remember anything, how could you remember you had amnesia?"

"Did you know it is impossible to erase yourself?"

Me: "Kinetic energy is energy of …?"

Student: "Kinetic"

"I hate fake peanut butter! It's not right!"

"Why doesn't our planet fall?"

"That ain't water, it's too stiff!"

"You can eat a million 'Lifesavers' and not one will save your life."

Student A: "What's the region that's way up north and way south?"

Student B: "Your Brain!"

After looking at some pictures of me from the 60s A student asked, "Mr.T, Was there no color when you were little?" I responded, "What?" He said, "Well all the pictures are in black and white."

Teacher: "From where do you get a DNA 'fingerprint'?"

Student: "From a person's finger."

"You can't drop stuff in distilled water because as soon as it hits the surface it will move."

"Cold is cold is cold and I'm cold!"

"Why does water taste so good when it doesn't have a flavor?"

"A catfish is like a cat and a fish."

"You can't get more 'rednecker' than that."

"You can't make waves, you're not Mr. Nature."

Student A: "If you come and get tutored what happens?"

Student B: "The teacher tutors you!"

I asked a class "Does anyone know why Jesse has been out?" A student responded, "She was here for like 2 weeks, just not in the same day though!"

"If African- Americans are from Africa is there such a place as 'Caucasia'?"

"If my parents ate me I'd cry!"

Me: "Let me make sure you've got the 'straight poop' on this assignment!"

Student: "What do you mean 'straight poop'?"

Me: "The right information!"

Student: "Well if 'poop' means information then our brains are full of 'poop'!"

Me: "She broke her wrist?"

Student: "Well, right now it's fractured but it might be broken."

"If adding too much water is called 'watered down' then shouldn't adding too little be called 'watered up'?"

"Mr. Troxel, if you eat animal crackers or gummy worms does that make you a non-vegetarian?"

"He's cute but he's ugly!"

"I know the definitions; I just don't know the words."

Me: "How did everyone do on this quiz?"

Student: "Mr. Troxel, I would've made a hundred, I knew all the answers they just weren't right."

Me: "Why do plants need CO_2?"

Student A: "To Breathe!"

Student B: "Plants don't breathe they inhale oxygen."

"Did humans survive the Ice Age?"

Me: "If you are racing in the Daytona 500 all you care about is that 500 miles; nothing before, nothing after."

Student: "Wait! They call it that because it's 500 miles?"

Me: "What is the law of supply and demand?"

Student: "Ain't that the haves and the have nots?"

"Does a piece of paper weigh more crumpled up or as a sheet?"

"Mr. T you laugh at the most amusing things."

"I thought nature was natural."

"Don't be acting stupid because with me it's not acting."

"I've found that hot sauce burns my mouth."

"I just want to know the things I don't know."

After trying banana pudding a student said, "I didn't like it… it tasted like bananas."

"People say you can't live without love but I think oxygen is more important."

"Can you get brain damage by talking too fast?"

"How come you sit on your butt but it still gets cold?"

"Pizza in English is like the same thing in Spanish."

"Horses don't walk on two legs as good as they walk on four."

"Mr. Troxel, guess what? I just looked at the periodic table and they're all in order."

"A young lady was putting rubber bands on her braces and informed me that, "These taste like rubber." (Who'd a thunk?)

Me: "Math and science are inseparable."

Student: "That don't mean I got to do it."

"I didn't tell a lie… I just didn't tell the truth."

"Mr. Troxel is there an equation to be happy?"

"Hey Trox – Did you know if you don't want to be naked you can just put socks on your feet?"

"She had an allergic reaction to an allergy."

"Fish go to the bathroom underwater."

"Bill Gates is so rich he can get stupid now."

Student: "Isn't alpha a type of fish?"

Me: "Not that I know of."

Student: "Well a beta is!"

"I don't remember where I was born."

* * * * *

I love it when a student gets tongue-tied (or 'brain-tied'). They don't seem to have any 'brakes' for their mouths, so 'verbal train wrecks' are inevitable.

"You made me lose my thought of train!"

"I got a 64 on 'thitical crinking'!" (Critical Thinking)

"Isn't ohm the noise you make when you're migrating?"

"If someone pokes you too hard in the belly button it can hurt your 'intestineys'."

"This is stuff from all week last year."

"Did you eat your coffee?"

"What's Jupiter? Not the planet I mean... never mind."

"I 'plid' the 'feeth'!"

"I speak 'fluid' French!"

"Mr. Troxel, That girl just used 'profoundity'."

"He broke my paper!"

"I have detention... I have to stay until three – o – ten!"

"I'm 'psythic'!" (Yes you are!)

"I have a creek in my back."

Teacher: "You have to prove yourself selfless."

Student A: "I 'm not selfish."

Student B: "It's sailfish! You know, like a sail and a fish."

"You can't play cards? You mean I can't play Goldfish?"

"It's in low orth earbit"

"Coffee stunts your gruff."

"I got a 'tension tantrum' at home."

"I'm not 'acusating' anybody."

"Do you like 'tobacco' sauce?"

"It's a 'laptop'? I thought it was a 'labtop'!"

I found a student's progress report on the floor and handed it to her. She responded, "Oh that fell out of my butt."

On a multiple choice test question the choices were A, B, C, D. A student answered "G".

"Mr. Troxel, every time I see the 'Calvin Cycle' I want to write Calvin Klein."

"When does the end of the story start?"

Student A: "We're like two pods in a pea!"

Student B: "You mean two peads in a pod!"

A student was explaining why his cousin was in the hospital: "He bleeds a lot so he has to get RVs."

A student asked me what stupendous meant. After I defined the word she declared,

"I feel stupidious!"

Students were discussing an incident in the cafeteria until one exclaimed,

"Let's not talk about vomification!"

Student A: "She took my 'crowns'!"

Student B: "You mean 'cranes'!"

Me: "That would be crayons!"

"I got "angra manager" issues." (Yes you do!)

Student: "I sawed it?"

Me: "That's not proper English."

Student: "OK I seened it."

"Mr. Troxel, That boy tried to touch my generals!"

"That girl talks like a million minutes a second."

Me: "Do you know what gumbo means?"

Student: "That's them oversized shrimp."

"Are you still grading our testesees?"

"Hush, they be singing the onomatopoeia!"

(Alma Mater)

Student A: "Mr. Troxel's a preacher!"

Student B: "No he's a pasture!"

"I got 'exemplimary' on my English test."

"I have a credit card… it's Caption America!"

* * * * *

There are some things students say that make you feel sorry for them and their parents. In the south we simply reply "Bless his heart!" The understood part of the phrase is, "He can't help it!" So when you read the following quotes don't forget to say (out loud) "Bless his heart. He can't help it!"

"Mr. Troxel, I thought I was going blind in my left eye, but come to find out the eye drops I was using was Super Glue."

"You've got to go to college to be a teacher? No Way!"

"What time is one twenty?"

I asked the class to define atomic bond. A blonde young lady blurted out, "That's atoms mating or something like that."

The same student came in the next day sporting a fresh tan. I asked, "Did you go to the beach yesterday?" She said, "No, I went to the tanning

51

bed." I cautioned her about too much UV exposure and she asked, "Why? What can it cause?" I told her, "Skin cancer for one thing." She said, "I don't have cancer." To which I said, "Yet!" She then said, "What's the difference between that and a tattoo? It's all under the skin." (Bless her heart!)

"Mr. Troxel, I just realized that a 'P' upside down and backwards is a 'd'."

"I have flamboyant cheeks... you know when they stretch they might go back."

"This woman had twins by two different men... they are internal twins."

"Mr. T wouldn't getting shocked just affect your blood pressure not your brain?"

"Mr. Troxel, can you get blind from reading with the lights off?"

"If someone is on life-support and you pull the plug then put it back in will they still die?"

Student: "Mr. Troxel, if you put a cow in the refrigerator would the milk freeze?

Me: "No, but you'll have a great milkshake!"

Student: "Really?"

While I was injured a student suggested, "Mr. Troxel, you should put a boat motor on you wheelchair."

A student sprained her wrist and declared in class, "I tried to put a sock on it like a cast but it didn't work."

"Mr. T did you know you have to cook chicken before you eat it?"

"I want a dolphin to be our national bird!"

"These shoes are so comfortable but they are killing my feet."

"Mr. Troxel, Did you know it's not 'AL' steak sauce it's 'A-1'? I just found that out yesterday."

"I biologically changed my name."

Student A: "You had to shave your head?"

Teacher: "Yes"

Student B: "Were you bald?"

"Which one do you think would kill more, a deer if you hit them across the head or a cheese steak?"

"I just spelled my name wrong."

"Mr. Troxel, I stuck my finger in the fryer to see if the grease was hot and it sizzled."

"Isn't it a good thing to have a low IQ?"

"Can you be illegally blind? Doesn't that mean you can see?"

"I want to eat turtle soup but I don't want any turtle meat in it."

Student A: "It's the last game and it's homecoming."

Student B: "Is it home?"

A student and I were discussing feats of strength. I told him I had witnessed a man blow up a hot water bottle until it burst. He asked, "With his feet?"

"Is the continent connected to the ground?"

Me: "There are complete mountain ranges underwater."

Student: "How come you can't see them?"

Teacher: "Any questions?"

Student A: "What does brothel mean?"

Teacher: "It's a house of prostitution."

Student B: "Oh, I have one!"

Student C: "You have a house of prostitution? That's gross!"

Student B: "No, I have a question."

Student C: "Oh, OK!"

"My mom can speak fluent 'Jibberish'."

A student said she was working out every day. I asked, "Have you done aerobics?" she replied, "We don't swim."

"Mr. Troxel, They say if you pee in your face it will something."

"How old are you when you're born?"

"Does anybody else feel like it's Thursday... even though it is?"

"Mr. Troxel, how come when you yawn it burns your nose?"

"I heard Eskimos call bubble-gum, 'nuki-nuki - yum-yums'!"

"Middle school was straight my first sixth grade year."

"Mr. Troxel, he said 'eat, eat' that's a double negative."

"I thought my foot was having a seizure."

"My head is small… sometimes."

A student came running in my room all upset and blurted, "Mr. Troxel, is it true a dog with no legs ran away." (Yes I laughed)

"If you're brain dead do you know what's going on?"

"Mr. Troxel, is a duck a rodent?"

"Did I squeeze my blood so hard that it popped off?"

"My arm just got light-headed."

I ran into a student I had not seen in a while at a local pizza restaurant so I asked where he had been.

Student: "I got kicked out of school."

Me: "For What?"

Student: "Fighting"

Me: "That will get you hurt"

Student: "Not me I'm invisible!"

"Mr. T, Did you know in some countries you have to pay for air to breathe?"

A young lady walked in my room all grins and giggles, so I asked, "Do you have a new boy friend?"

She beamed from ear to ear and said, "Yeah!"

My next question was only natural, "What's his name?"

She responded with that 14 year old smitten voice, "Trent". I then asked, "What's his last name?" She didn't know.

While out shopping with my family a student walked in the Ralph Lauren Outlet store and said to me, "They have Polo here?"

"Mr. Troxel if you go into space how does your brain work up there?"

Student: "Can we draw on our lab report?"

Me: "You can include an illustration."

Student: "But you said to draw a conclusion."

"If you threw a bowling ball out of an airplane wouldn't it get stuck in a cloud?"

Me: "There are small amounts of iron in your blood."

Student A: "I don't have metal inside me."

Student B: "Well duh! You're not a robot."

"30 cents is more than a quarter right?"

"Mr. Troxel yesterday my doctor wanted to know when my last lab work was. I told him tomorrow… we are doing a lab today right?"

Me: "The man who did Einstein's autopsy kept his brain."

Student A: "Was he decapitated?"

Student B: "Is it still good?"

Me: "Have you ever boiled water?"

Student: "What happens if you catch it on fire?"

"Can you be allergic to light?"

"So a mime goes through his whole life and never says a word?"

Halfway through a class a student asked, "Mr. Troxel can I take my book back? I left my locker open."

Me: "What does the prefix 'milli' mean?

Student: "A bunch."

"The sun turns into the moon at night."

"If everyone in the entire world breathed at the same time would the CO_2 kill us?"

"Are you still alive when your heart's not in you?"

"I didn't feel like shaving my legs yesterday so I put duct tape on them like wax… I think it took off some skin."

"I thought you said this was an assessment not a test!"

"I'm going to get the hiccups on purpose so I can grow taller."

"I thought I had cancer yesterday, but in 6h period it went away."

"If you give someone AIDS do you have to marry them?"

"I'm really starting to like my new boyfriend."

"I am dumb!"

"A Mini Cooper is faster than a 73 Mach 1 Mustang."

"You know a lot of people have the same last name. Are there not enough names to go around?"

"I got a sunburn and burnt all the freckles off my nose."

Video: "Hikers found the remains of a man 5,300 years old."

Student: "Was he still alive?"

"Are the blue guys (in Blue Man Group) born blue?"

I told my students that I was officiating a former student's wedding the following weekend. One young lady asked, "Mr. Troxel did you do your own wedding?"

* * * * *

"A mind is a terrible thing to waste"

As a teacher I understand that parents do not keep their good students at home. We get the best they've got. There are times however when one must wonder where these kids come up with things. They certainly do not think before they speak. On occasion I even wonder if they've thought at all.

Student A: Mr. Troxel, How many children do you have?

Me: I have five growing boys!

Student B: Good Lord! You have 10 kids?

I was helping a student with some math homework problems. I asked, "What times 2 equals 10?" She said, "20".

Student A: Does ham come from pigs?

Me: Yes

Student B: It ain't pork though!

Student C: I thought beef came from pigs!?

Student: "Mr. Troxel your kids are cute."

Me: "I think so but I'm biased."

Student: "What's that mean? Are you bisexual?"

"How do you make dry ice? Do you like blow dry it without melting it?"

Teacher: "Whose picture is on the twenty dollar bill?"

Student: "Thomas Edison"

While reviewing for a test on organic compounds I told the class, "You will need to know what fats are." A student raised his hand and asked, "Is that with a 'ph' or an 'f'?"

One day I was calling out letters of a matching section for a homework assignment so I said "L". A student didn't understand so I use the phonetic alphabet and said "Lima". The student replied, "That's an animal!"

"If my voice goes hoarse it's because I'm turning into leukemia."

A baseball player once said, "I caught an amazing catch!" So I said, "So you didn't catch the ball?" He replied, "No, I caught a catch!"

A couple of months later the same student proclaimed to the class, "I had the most beautiful interception playing basketball last night!"

"I want to speak Hebrew…That's a language right?"

"This is Biology? I thought you were a science teacher!"

"Mr. Troxel, Have you ever chewed minty gum so hard that you feel the burn in your eye?"

Student A: "Mr. Troxel, can a mango die of internal bleeding?"

Student B: "A mango, isn't that an animal?"

Me: "I'm going to the beach tomorrow!"

Student: "You're gonna get stung by those 'jelly-rays'!"

"After Mozart died he threw himself I the river."

While working a problem on the board I asked the class what 3 times 3 equals. In unison the class said "6".

"Mr. Troxel, can you selectively breed plastic?"

Student: "My grandpa is 103 today."

Me: "103 and still living, wow!"

Student: "Well he used to be but he's not anymore."

"Mr. Troxel, Did you know you swallow 2 million spiders every time you sleep?"

"That makes me itch when I see other people with feet!"

Student A: "I thought Cinco-de-Mayo was mayonnaise."

Student B: "No it means goodbye!"

"Are dust bunnies animals or just dust?"

"Can humans molt?"

"Mr. Troxel, is cheese cow meat?"

When asked to give the date for a particular discovery the student asked, "Are we in BC or AD?"

"Mr. Troxel, Is 'Duck Tape' really made of duck?"

Teacher: "What are the three types of pulleys?"

Student: "Fixed, moveable, and broken towel."

"Do farmers breed turkeys with pigs to make turkey bacon?"

"Mr. Troxel, this weekend a dead deer bit me!"

"It's 12 o'clock when the compass points north!"

"Siberia... Isn't that in Africa?"

Student A: "Dirt is spelled D-A-R-T!"

Student B: "You forgot the 'E'... dart is spelled D-A-R-T-E!"

"I have an aphobic on my tongue"

* * * * *

It is easy to blame teachers for students not learning basic skills. However when a student has made it to high school there are some things they should know by virtue of sitting in a desk for 9 years. In fact just living 13 plus years should provide a certain amount of information. Sometimes your only response is to shake your head.

"Negative 3 plus positive 3 is 6 right?"

"Is the homecoming game at home or away?"

"It's 'I' before 'C' except after 'P'!"

"Do you have to go to college to play the 'Geetar'?"

A student walked up to my desk to turn in a late assignment. The follow exchange ensued:

Student A: "I was told I could turn this in late."

Me: "You were deceived."

Student A: "I'm not dead!"

Student B: "He said deceived not descend."

Student C: "No it's conceived."

Student D: "Who got pregnant?"

Student E: "I thought that was desist."

"The square root of 3 is 9"

Student: "I missed less than 3."

Me: "So how many did you miss?"

Student: "I missed 5."

"I'm not a sophomore, I'm a 10th grader!"

"Did you know a pickle and a cucumber are the same thing?"

"If we speak English why do we have to learn it?"

Me: "Have you ever heard the song, 'Great Balls of Fire'?"

Student: "Isn't that AC/DC?"

"Does gravity still work when it's cold?"

"Mr. Troxel, Can you be related to like... an animal?"

Student A: "Just because the Sun goes down doesn't mean it's not there!"

Student B: "So that means the moon is there too?"

"How do calculators know this stuff without thinking?"

"If you like freeze yourself could you live?"

Me: "What's 2 times 1?"

Student: "3"

Answer written on the dry erase board:

"2 + 2 = 2"

"Mr. Troxel, don't pharmacy and fireman start

with the same letter?"

"You can't hang upside down 'cause all the blood will rush to your head and you'll drowned."

"Wait! You said yes you may and it's not even may yet."

"Mr. Troxel someone said there are 50 states but that's not right because Pluto was determined not to be a planet."

-----

* * * * *

No one wants to get in trouble. In fact I don't know of anyone who enjoys negative consequences. Yet it still amazes me some of the excuses students use to try in order to stay out of trouble:

"It's not my fault I wanted to write a letter to my friend!"

When asked why he didn't turn in an assignment a student replied, "I brought it in today yesterday!"

"Only my eyes were sleeping. I heard every word you said."

Me: "You cheated on the last test."

Student: "I can't 'rememberize' that."

Me: "Did you throw that?"

Student: "No! See that! He's got a flying ball in his hand!"

Teacher: "Why are you late?"

Student: "I got to pee so bad my head hurt!"

* * * * *

The following quotes probably should have made me burst into laughter; alas they did not. Instead I found myself at a complete loss for words and could almost hear crickets chirping in my ears.

Teacher: "It's a movie not a game."

Student: Same difference

Teacher: 'A movie requires no interaction from you; you simply watch it."

Student: "They both come in a case though!"

"Way to shorten my day longer man!"

"I thought dogs had 7 lives."

"The air conditioning is burning the side of my arm."

"When you're like going to the bathroom and you're doing #2... if you touch your eye you get pink-eye"

"Did you see your face?"

"I'm gonna try and pull my brain out of my nose."

"A paper towel is made of paper right?"

"When you say favorite music you mean the genreneric?"

"Can you bag acid rain?"

"I'm a smart retard!"

"Mr. Troxel, isn't the government in your TV watchin' your every move?"

"Why would the moon ever be yellow? Nobody can pee that far."

"I wish boogers weren't invented."

"What makes chocolate allergic to dogs?"

"Can you break your eyeball?"

"You shouldn't eat seafood overnight… you'll get seasick!"

"Mr. Troxel you know how you can tan with the sun? Well can you tan with the moon?"

"Mr. T, Have you ever eaten fried butter?"

"I couldn't get stuck inside my own locker… I know the combination."

"How does your hair connect to your brain?"

"Only eight months till I graduate… that's a whole pregnancy."

"If I become president one day, everyone is chopping their feet off except for mine."

"The hiccups are blocking my breathing snout."

"Instead of being 4'11 ½" she makes 4'12" this year."

"This book smells like paper."

"Donkeys don't have ears Mr. Troxel!"

Student: "Mr. Troxel I lost my locker combination; where do I get it?

Me: "Student Information Desk"

Student: "Do they have it?"

"Narcissist isn't that like someone who plays with fire?"

"Can you make me copies of computer paper?"

"Was that back in a day when gas was 100 cent?"

"I hate coffee... It's burnt water!"

****

I consider myself fairly adept at keeping up with terms the student use. However, there are times when I really need an interpreter.

"He put dat mug on you dog! Who he be muggin'?"

"My 'filipiak' hurts!"

"My 'itearitnatin' ain't workin' this morning."

"I'm going to fall down the 'coilin'."

"I 'box' you in the 'feece'."

"Everybody got swag but swag got me."

"You knock the breath out of my water."

The following is a student's response to a question on a lab report exactly as it was written (punctuation and all):

"The final temperatures of a mixture of two liquids affected by the starting temperatures o f the liquids were because of the temperature of the final temperature and the starting temperature would not go to change the temperature higher or lower then the final or starting. That means that when the final and starting temperature are mixture the temperature would not be more then the other."

The only thing I could write on his paper was- WHAT??????

"There's 5 Fridays, 5 Saturdays, and 5 Sundays this month. That only happens every 8 – 23rd of October."

"You ack like you must be wasn't writtin'!"

"Don't be talkin' about that clastroniphobic stuff"?

* * * * *

Students seem to say and worry about things that are just plain weird. Since I am weird I think I am qualified to judge weird. But some of this stuff weirds me out...Is that weird?

"If a fish swims upside down will it drown?"

Student A: "Sounds like jingle bells."

Student B: "What the Frisbee?"

Student C: "Tis a slinky."

"Mr. Troxel did you know if a person is dead and you stab that person, you will go to jail for murder because it's a second murder."

"If you committed suicide would you get arrested?"

"I wish I could take my toes off so I could bite my toenails."

"Collard greens make you have butts."

"Is salt water like whale sperm?"

"If you pour acid in your ears does it make your ears bubble?"

"Don't ducks have 3 feet?"

Student A: "I don't eat anything that can't walk away."

Student B: "So you don't eat cow?"

Student A: "I mean after it is cooked."

"Turtles can breathe out their buttholes underwater... that's why you see the trail of bubbles."

"So if you're in Hawaii and a volcano erupts and the lava burns you... wouldn't you hurt after 5 minutes when the nerves kick in?"

"You can surgically become a Doctor."

Me: "What's your favorite color?"

Student: "Clear"

"You can drown in your pillow."

"Mr. Troxel, if I smile in the sun will my teeth tan?"

"My birth parents are Russian and I was born in Russia but my parents who adopted me are real people."

Student A: "I drink hairspray every day"

Student B: "Wouldn't that make your insides stick together?"

Student A: "Only if it's Aquanet."

A young lady was looking at pictures of my former students. She pointed at one who was Miss Teen SC and said, "Is she real?"

"So can you grow mushrooms on your feet?"

"I want to take marine biology next year so I can digest things."

"Everyone calls me Christian... Do you see a 'tn'?"

Teacher: "The answer is zero."

Student A: "Isn't zero invisible?"

Student B: "No stupid, 1 is invisible."

"I just choked on steam"

Opening up a freezer a student said, "Look! Cold Steam!"

"It's like when you're driving and the sun follows you home."

"When pee drops from a plane why does it freeze?"

"I know a man can be a cow!"

"Mr. Troxel – So when you're dead all of a sudden you hear a bang."

"There's still a bunch of oxygen in my nose that's why I can't breathe."

Me: "The next day we have off will be February 17, three weeks from now."

Student: "Will we be in school then? Will I be in 9th or 10th grade?"

"Are buffalo wings chicken or buffalo?"

"If math was a person I would kill it."

"If I was a man I'd date myself!"

"My jacket smells like Hello Kitty."

"My mom threw a waffle at me."

"Mr. Troxel isn't it true that when a fart comes out of your butt the air is brown... I mean I know you can't see it but it's brown."

****

Young people often have no grasp of age. They think their 25 year old brother is ancient. So when they ponder that I taught their sibling or even their mother... they think I should be in a rest home.

"Did they do scientific stuff when you were a kid?"

"What was an Ipod in the 70's like?"

Referring to our town's mayor of 20+ years a student said, "Who's that man who is so old... I think he invented Summerville."

Student: "How old are you?"

Me: 16 with 32 years of experience."

Student: "So you're like 70?"

Me: Next time we have something fun planned."

Student: "Our kind of fun or your kind of fun?"

"They've been married 12 years… why aren't they dead?"

"Was baseball invented when you were a kid?"

Student: "Mr. Troxel why is everyone congratulating you?"

Me: "I just finished my masters."

Student: "Masters… like the golf Masters?"

In March of 2014 the following conversation occurred.

Me: "My birthday is March 25, 1964."

Student A: "So you're like 100?"

Student B: "He's 34."

****

Religion in the public school

The US Supreme Court ruled in 1962 to remove religion (prayer) from schools. However, students often like to ask questions or make comments about God and the Bible that really make you think we might want to reconsider that call!

"I just realized the Virgin Mary was a virgin!"

"I drink wine every Sunday, my church takes community."

"Is Christmas on the 21st or 25th this year?"

"I thought aqueous meant you worship the devil."

Student: "How long has it been since Jesus was born?"

Me: "About two thousand years."

Student: "No way, it has to be way past 9000 years 'cause it was 1999 a few years ago."

After learning that I am a pastor a student asked me where my church met. I told him "We meet in a strip mall." His friend exclaimed, "You preach in a strip club?"

* * * * *

I think it's time to bring back maps and colored pencils. Geography doesn't seem to be registering with our little angels.

"What's Indiana? Is it a state?"

Student A: "Isn't the Rocky Mountains in North Carolina?"

Student B: "No that's Tennessee"

"Do people live in Egypt?"

"Washington DC is in a different country."

(How True!)

Student A: "What did you do this weekend Mr. Troxel?"

Me: "I went to Virginia Beach for a wedding!"

Student A: "Virginia Beach? That's like in Virginia?"

Student B: "There are no beaches in Virginia! Are you crazy?"

Student C: "Yeah, Virginia doesn't have an ocean."

"When you put your finger on a map and touch a state are you touching the actual state?"

"Isn't Cuba part of the United States?"

"Europe is in America right?"

"Connecticut reminds me of pineapple."

"Hey I'm Irish from that Irish place."

"Isn't Cuba in Canada?"

Me: "Stop talking to him!"

Student: "He's teaching me how to speak Mexican."

Me: "No, he speaks Spanish."

Student: "He's from Mexico he speaks Mexican. We're from 'American' and we speak American don't we?"

Most of the class in unison: "We speak English!"

Keeping in mind we live near Charleston SC and its beautiful beaches:

"What ocean are we near? We swim in the Pacific ocean right?"

"I need to go to the British."

Student A: "I thought the Grand Canyon was in Canada."

Student B: "I thought it was in Nebraska or someplace like that."

Student C: "Nevada is in California."

The substitute for my class one day was a naturalized US citizen from Colombia. When I returned the following conversation ensued:

Student A: "He was Egyptian or something."

Me: "No he is Colombian."

Student B: "No he's Hispanic"

Student C: "Columbia South Carolina?"

Student D: "That Asian guy was weird."

Student E: "You mean that Iraqi substitute we had yesterday?"

* * * * *

There are 15 state abbreviations on the Periodic Table of Elements. Each year I give the students and assignment to find them for extra credit. I am surprised every year over how some of our "50-nifty" are spelled and the additional "states" I did not learn about when I was in school.

Abbreviation	State Name
Lu	Lussiana
Ci	Cinnunati
Mg	Montgumary
Ne	New Mexico
No	Norway
Fe	Florida
Fr	France
In	Indianapolis
At	Atlanta
Uuh	Utah

* * * * *

"Those who don't know history are doomed to repeat it!" Or perhaps at least repeat a grade.

"Ronald Reagan.... Was that a president?"

Teacher: "What happened in 1942?"

Student A: "The Civil War"

Teacher: "Again, what happened in 1942?"

Student B: "I know, Vietnam!"

Student C: "Columbus sailed the ocean blue."

Me: "China is a communist country."

Student: "That means there aren't no people there."

"Was there ever a mayor of the United States?"

"The best President this country ever had was Martin Luther King Jr.!"

Teacher: "Who is our current president?" (2003)

Student: "Bill Bush"

Student A: "Who did Princess Diana marry?"

Me: Prince Charles

Student A: "What is he the prince of?"

Me: "He's the Prince of Wales."

Student B: "So they got married in the ocean?"

* * * * *

With all this confusion even I have a little brain malfunction on occasion. I cannot find humor in students' comments if I don't admit to a few of my own.

Student: "What would happen if nuclear bomb was dropped near here?"

Me: "There will be a bunch of dead people walking around."

Student: "Why do we need to get up so early?"

Me: "That's because you have to be here before the turkey crows."

Student: "Mr. T, you have a beer belly."

Me: "I don't have a 'Beer Gelly'!"

"He just went to sleep and woke up dead."

* * * * *

I hope you had a few good laughs or at least a smile or two. Please remember,

Since other people laugh at you, you might as well join in on the fun!

- MCT

About the Author

MC Troxel lives Summerville SC with his wife of 27 years and his 5 sons. He teaches Physical Science at Summerville High School and is associate pastor at Lowcountry Baptist Church.

Born in Charleston on March 25, 1964, Mike loves his home state and has learned the importance of laughter in life and not taking himself too seriously. He says, "Since other people laugh at you, you might as well join in on the fun!"

Mike holds a BS in Education from The Citadel (1986), a Master of Christian Education from Andersonville Theological Seminary (2009) and a Master of Education Administration from Grand Canyon University (2012).

What teachers and students have to say about *Mr. Troxel is it true bacteria eat you alive when you're dead.*

'These comments are too funny to be made up!'

Risa F. *Physical Science Teacher*

"Hilarious! I wish I had done this when I first started teaching!"

Jill R. *Math Teacher*

"How can you not get at least a giggle at these stories."

Sarah H. *Chemistry Teacher*

"Some of these kids had to be on something, otherwise it's just sad."

Raven *11th grade student*

"Awesome! A Hilarious Glimpse into the Teenage Mind!"

Tommy W. *Physical Science Teacher*

"I loved reading this book. I have bought copies for family, friends, and fellow educators, who have all laughed out loud from the very first page."

Kent F. *Math Teacher*

Made in the USA
Charleston, SC
05 June 2016